God
is
calling
you
to
be
fearless
and
to

**Fear
LESS**

God
is
calling
you
to
be
fearless
and
to
Fear
LESS

Marta E. Greenman

Maureen H. Maldonado

© 2023 by Marta E. Greenman and Maureen H. Maldonado

Published by Words of Grace & Truth, PO Box 860223, Plano, TX 75086. (469) 854-3574

Words of Grace & Truth is honored to present this title in partnership with the authors. The views expressed or implied in this work are those of the authors. Words of Grace & Truth provides our imprint seal representing design excellence, creative content, and high quality production.

No part of this publication may be reproduced, stored in a retrieval system, or transmitted in any way by any means—electronic, mechanical, photocopy, recording, or otherwise—without the prior permission of the copyright holder, except as provided by USA copyright law.

The authors have permission to use all the versions noted in *FearLESS: God is Calling You to be Fearless and to FearLESS*.

Scripture quotations taken from the New American Standard Bible © Copyright 1960, 1962, 1963, 1968, 1971, 1972, 1973, 1975, 1977, 1995, 2020 by The Lockman Foundation. Used by permission.

IISBN softcover Color: 978-1-960575-06-7

ISBN Hardcover Color: 978-1-960575-07-4

ISBN softcover Black & White: 978-1-960575-09-8

ISBN ePub: 978-1-960575-15-9

ISBN Mobi: 978-1-960575-08-1

Library of Congress Catalog Number: 2023904861

ACKNOWLEDGMENTS

Thank you, Marta Greenman, for your friendship, guidance, and trust in inviting me to write this devotional with you and for all you have taught me along the way.

Ray Maldonado, I so appreciate the care you gave me when I was ill with COVID-19 in the early days of writing.

Heidi and Hayley, you are truly the best daughters anyone ever had. I thank you for your love and laughter and editing.

Cody, Carlee, Dustin, and Eliza, you fill my heart with joy!

I am nothing without You, Lord. Words cannot express how humbled I am to be able to work on something for You!

Maureen H. Maldonado

Special thanks to Colleen Sand, Cody Ogg, Maggie Wehunt, Heather Speck, Haley Ferguson, Tara Swinford for your photography contributions.

Maureen, you are a treasured friend, colaborer, and accountability partner. What a joy to get to "do life" with you. I can't wait to see what the Lord has in store for the next ten years!

Marshall, you always support me 100 percent. Thank you for always being by my side.

Mom, you have instilled in me a can-do, adventurous spirit. I am so grateful to be your daughter. You are a gift.

As always, without the Lord, I am nothing. I pray to be counted worthy of the ministry to which You have called me.

Marta E. Greenman

CONTENTS

Introducing Marta and Maureen	ix
Authors' Note	xiii
Section 1: Old Testament	xv
Yārē'	17
Our Story: In the Steep, Foggy Albanian Mountains	18
The Emotion of Fear	21
Day 1: Smoldering Stubs (Isaiah 7:4)	23
Day 2: Rod and Staff (Psalm 23:4)	27
Day 3: God Hears Us (Genesis 21:17)	31
Day 4: I Am Your Shield (Genesis 15:1)	35
Day 5: Signs from God (Joshua 1:9)	39
Day 6: Red Sea Moments (Exodus 14:13–14)	43
Day 7: Protection (Psalm 23:4)	47
Intellectual Anticipation of Evil	51
Day 8: Watch Your Feet (Proverbs 3:25)	53
Day 9: Fear Is a Tactic (Isaiah 41:10)	57
Day 10: Treasures (Genesis 43:23)	61
Day 11: Confident (Psalm 27:3)	65
Day 12 : Call on the Lord (Lamentations 3:57)	69
Reverence or Awe	73
My Story: Heavenly Father vs. Earthly Father	75
Day 13: This Is Only a Test (Genesis 22:12)	77
Day 14: Wisdom (1 Samuel 12:14)	81

Righteous Behavior, or Piety	85
Day 15: Midwives (Exodus 1:20–21)	87
Day 16 : 911 Prayer (Nehemiah 6:9)	91
Day 17: Correction Equals Change (Job 11:15)	95
Formal Religious Worship	99
Day 18: Battle Cry (Nehemiah 4:14)	101
Yir'a	105
Day 19: Fear God, Not Man (Nehemiah 5:15)	107
Day 20: Fear of the Lord (Psalm 111:10)	111
Day 21: Fools Hate Knowledge (Proverbs 1:28–29)	115
Bālah	119
My Story: Romanian Train Station	120
Day 22: Recognize the Fiery Darts (Ezra 4:4)	123
Měgôrâ	127
Our Story: My New BFF	129
Day 23: Faith or Fear (Psalm 34:4)	131
Day 24: Deliverer (Psalm 34:4)	135
Day 25: The Same God (Isaiah 66:4)	139
Section 2: New Testament	143
Deiliaō	145
Day 26: The Gift of Peace (John 14:27)	147
Merimnaō	151
My Story: The Day the Earth Moved	152
Day 27: Anxiety (Philippians 4:6)	155
Phobeo	159
My Story: Blessings on the Porch	160
Day 28: No Hostages (Luke 12:32)	161
Day 29: Jesus Holds the Keys (Revelation 1:17–18)	165
Day 30: Be Ready (Luke 2:10)	169

Introducing Marta and Maureen

Marta Greenman

Marta left corporate America in 1998 to become a staff missionary with a church-planting organization known today as e3Partners. She led American churches in planting new ones with international church partners. During this period, Marta spent much of her time in the field on evangelism and discipleship, traveling to Colombia, Mexico, Moldova, Peru, Romania, Ukraine, Venezuela, and Zimbabwe. She also had the privilege of leading women's conferences in biblical training.

Marta began teaching inductive Bible studies in 1997 at her home church, where she taught faithfully for fifteen years. Debbie Stuart, the former women's ministry director, said, "Marta Greenman is a master teacher, weaving biblical principles, personal stories, and clear application with every lesson. She walks in truth, loves the Word, and has dedicated her life to teaching that truth to women."

After seven years on the mission field in Romania, Marta began to write Bible study curriculum. Her first study, *Bound to Be Free*, was published in 2011. Marta founded Words of Grace

& Truth in May 2011, a ministry devoted to teaching God's Word to the nations and teaching others to do the same, using curriculum God birthed through her teaching ministry. Since then, *Leaders, Nations, and God* and *ACTs420NOW* have been published. Her fourth book is a thirty-day devotional entitled *FearLESS*, co-authored with Maureen Maldonado. She continues to write additional biblically based materials.

Marta's latest ministry venture is GraceAndTruthRadio.World (GTRW), a global radio station outreach with God's message of grace and truth. Her program *Under God*, with co-host Maureen Maldonado, airs on GTRW Mondays at 3:30 p.m. CST. Marta's passion, regardless of the nation where she may be, is teaching God's Word and equipping others to teach. She is a gifted teacher, speaker, and expositor of God's Word. Marta lives in the Dallas–Fort Worth area of Texas with her husband of almost thirty years.

Maureen Maldonado

Maureen is the second of seven children. Growing up in a home where worldly wealth was a foreign concept, she always felt treasured by her parents and knew she was rich in love. Maureen married young and raised two amazing daughters. Her grandchildren are a blessing beyond anything she could imagine. Recently, she was able to add a granddaughter-in-love who adds joy to the mix.

Maureen has a master's degree in education from California State University and spent her career as a teacher, vice-principal, and principal in elementary education. Maureen never planned to leave California or the education system, but God had other plans.

After Maureen's husband was transferred to Arizona in 2006 and then to Texas in 2011, she spent several years teaching Just Moved, a Christian-based ministry program developed by Susan Miller for women who are moving home due to life changes (https://justmoved.org). God used her teaching education and experience as a training ground to begin teaching for Him.

Involved in Bible studies in California, Arizona, and Texas, Maureen grew exponentially in her faith, love of God, and His Word. The culmination of these experiences led her to co-host the radio program *Under God* on GraceAndTruthRadio.World, where God's Word is taught to the nations.

Today Maureen is using her new-to-her method of studying the Bible and her long-applied teaching methods to teach the next generation of believers. Her prayer is for others to gain as much insight into God's transformational Word as she has received. She describes it as "opening the shades and letting in all the sunlight on a gloomy day." Maureen feels honored and humbled to be a part of Words of Grace & Truth and asks others to join in prayer for this needed ministry and for the church, our country, and our world.

Maureen and her husband, Raymond, reside in Texas, where they have transplanted almost their entire family from California.

AUTHORS' NOTE

Dear Reader,

Fear and faith cannot occupy the same space.

Today, the world is filled with plenty of opportunities to be fearful. As believers in Jesus Christ, we are to be overcomers and walk by faith. We need to learn to be fearLESS.

Over the coming days, we will look at healthy and unhealthy fears. A healthy fear of danger keeps us away from poisonous snakes or sharp cliffs without guardrails. An unhealthy fear of the world's opinions leads us to consider man's views or desires more important than God's principles and precepts. Our goal in this study is to show you how the fear of the Lord gives us boldness to lead the victorious life we are called to by Christ.

We have divided this devotional according to Old and New Testament references as well as different Hebrew and Greek words. Some definitions, you will notice, have a stark difference in meaning while others are similar. Discovering the difference between an earthly fear versus a fear of the Lord is essential to a growing relationship with the Lord.

Our thirty-day devotional will focus mainly on the emotion of fear and reverence, or awe, of our Lord. We believe the more you fear God, the more your earthly fears will retreat as though in a rearview mirror. We trust your fears will become more distant as you draw closer to the Lord.

We hope each day of this devotional leads you to become a bit more FearLESS.

Consumed by His Call,

Marta E. Greenman *Maureen H. Maldonado*

SECTION ONE
Old Testament

Yārē'

Hebrew offers five different meanings for the word *yārē'*. Most often, the Old Testament uses the Hebrew word *yārē'* for *fear* 382 times.

In the *Theological Wordbook of the Old Testament*, we read:

The biblical usages of *yārē'* are divided into five general categories:

1) The emotion of fear,

2) The intellectual anticipation of evil without emphasis upon the emotional reaction,

3) Reverence or awe,

4) Righteous behavior, or piety,

5) Formal religious worship.[1]

Our devotional will examine each of these different usages of *yārē'*.

---

[1] Robert L. Harris, Gleason L. Archer Jr., and Bruce K. Waltke, "Essay," in *Theological Wordbook of the Old Testament* (Chicago: Moody Press, 1980) 399.

In the Steep, Foggy Albanian Mountains

Our Story: Part One

In 2013, I was part of a missionary team led by Marta ministering in the beautiful country of Albania. Nine of us, both Americans and Albanians, along with our American-sized luggage, piled into a van. It was dusk, and we were driving from Greece into Albania.

As night approached, the fog set in while our car began to climb the steep mountain pass. The road lacked lights and guardrails, and visibility was almost non-existent. We were on a two-way highway, but the width of the road barely accommodated one-and-a-half cars. When we realized it was very possible we could plummet down the side of the mountain at the slightest mistake by the driver, fear began to grip us. One of our team members held up her phone and began to play the song "The God of Angel Armies" by Chris Tomlin. We began to sing quietly of the God who is our sword and shield and who is always by our side in darkest night.

Our fears began to subside, and we chose God over fear. As we sang, God calmed our emotions and brought us all safely down the mountain.

Maureen

Our Story: Part Two

The Albanian leader was continually saying "Hurry up!" to us Americans. "We don't want to get caught on the top of the mountain." Of course, we had no idea why she was so insistent. This was our vacation day, and we wanted to spend our last moments soaking up sun and buying our earthly treasures to take home to our families and friends. We had no idea of the dangers awaiting us when fog set in on top of the mountain.

The American team consisted of five women, including a single mom and my mother. I had an irrational fear we would plummet down the mountain and everyone else would be killed, yet somehow I would survive. As the leader of the team, I would be obliged to face the families at home. I imagined informing two husbands their wives were gone and a little boy his mother was dead. I thought about how hard it would be to face my brother and sisters if my mother perished.

I'm so grateful God had His angel armies take us safely down the mountain so we could return to tell all that God did—in, through, and particularly for us—during our missionary adventure. *Marta*

Yārē'

יָרֵא

The Emotion of Fear

The *Theological Wordbook of the Old Testament* teaches, "Typical examples of fearing as an emotional reaction are the Jews' fear of the fires on Mount Sinai (Deut. 5:5) and the fear of the Jews at Mizpah when they heard of the Philistine mobilization (1 Sam. 7:7)."[2]

---

[2] Robert L. Harris, Gleason L. Archer Jr., and Bruce K. Waltke, "Essay," in *Theological Wordbook of the Old Testament* (Chicago: Moody Press, 1980), 399.

Day One

Smoldering Stubs

*Take care, and be calm, have no fear
and do not be fainthearted . . .*

Isaiah 7:4

A re you in the middle of a battle and afraid of the outcome?

In Isaiah 7, we read of a battle going on that threatened the existence of Jerusalem. The Old Testament has many examples of how God allowed His people to be overtaken because of their sin but only in God's time. Evil kings came and went and would get close to devouring Jerusalem; then God would step in at the last minute and provide a reprieve.

This time, two kings from the Northern Kingdom had come against King Ahaz (descendant of the house of David) and were camped outside Jerusalem with their armies. Neither side seemed to be winning.

Then God told the prophet Isaiah to deliver a message to King Ahaz: "Take care, and be calm, have no fear and do not be fainthearted because of these two stubs of smoldering firebrands, on account of the fierce anger of Rezin and Aram, and the son of Remaliah" (Isa. 7:4).

God told King Ahaz that he first needed to quiet his mind and be ready to listen to the good message he was about to receive. The message went on to tell King Ahaz not to be afraid of two evildoers (Rezin and Aram). His enemies were not fierce like a raging fire but mere stubs of 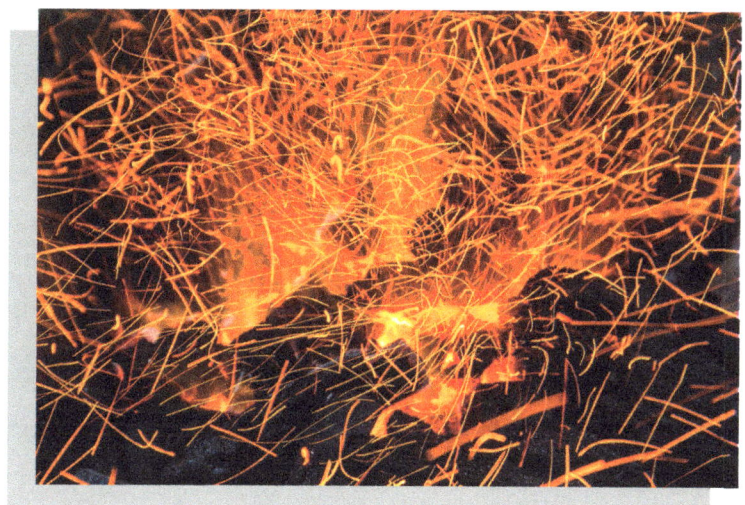 smoldering wood. They were more smoke than fire, and the fire could easily be extinguished.

Look at your own battles and fears. Are they really like a flaming fire or merely smoldering stubs? Do you have evil forces trying to enter and smash your personal kingdom? Remember the words God gave Isaiah for King Ahaz: quiet your mind and listen to the Lord, and have no fear of smoldering stubs. They are more smoke than fire and will burn themselves out quickly.

Reflection

Remember a time when your fears of a bad outcome were not realized. What lessons of faith did you learn?

....
....
....
....

What special verse ministered to you?

....
....
....
....

Do you have trouble being calm in the face of fear?

....
....
....
....

Would you call your fear an inferno or a smoldering stub? Why?

....
....
....

Day Two

Rod and Staff

Even though I walk through the valley of the shadow of death,
I fear no evil; for Thou art with me;
Thy rod and Thy staff, they comfort me.

Psalm 23:4

Have you been in a place of deep darkness?

Have you felt as if your world were tumbling down? During such times, it is easy to let fear engulf us.

As a shepherd boy, David knew these feelings all too well. He tells us clearly in Psalm 23:4 why he didn't fear: "Even though I walk through the valley of the shadow of death, I fear no evil; for Thou art with me; Thy rod and Thy staff, they comfort me." David didn't fear, because he knew the Lord was with him.

As a shepherd, David knew the benefits of the rod and the staff. He was comfortable with these tools. He could lean on his staff when he was tired and weary. He could also use it as a guide to keep the sheep from wandering off the path. David compared God to his staff. We need to lean on God when we encounter trials. We can trust our Savior to gently direct us when we are weary and tired from life's rocky encounters.

The rod was crooked, allowing the shepherd to rescue sheep from hazardous situations. The shepherd also used it to defend against wolves and other animals. David knew that God would pull him back from danger and defend him from his enemies.

As believers, we can have this same FearLESS attitude when we come upon life's inevitable valleys of the shadow of death. We just need to trust in our Savior's rod and staff for our protection. *Marta*

Reflection

What are you trusting in for your protection instead of God?

Do you need to change your perspective about God's rod and staff?

What steps do you need to take in order to adopt a fearLESS attitude?

Day Three

God Hears Us

God heard the lad crying;

and the angel of God called to Hagar from heaven

and said to her, "What is the matter with you, Hagar?

Do not fear, for God has heard the voice of the lad where he is."

Genesis 21:17

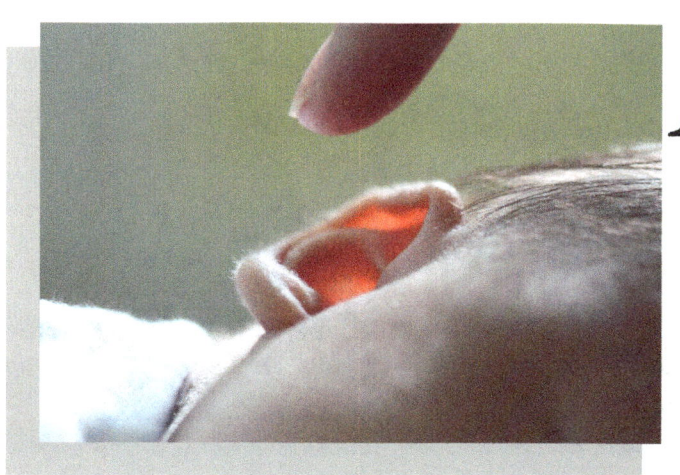

Hagar

was a woman

who lost everything.

This servant woman, who had borne a child by Abraham, her master, was thrown out of her home along with her son, Ishmael. Years earlier, God had told Abraham he would have a son and would become the father of many nations. When no son appeared, Abraham had a child with Hagar (Gen. 16). Abraham's wife, Sarah, was jealous and sent Hagar and her son to wander in the wilderness, giving them only a loaf of bread and a skin of water. Can you imagine her feelings of rejection, abandonment, and fear?

When the water ran out and no more food was to be found, Hagar placed her son far enough away so she would not hear his cries or watch him die. Then she "lifted up her voice and wept" (Gen. 21:16). Verse seventeen says God heard the crying and sent the angel of God, who told her, "Do not fear." The angel showed her a well, where they quenched their thirst. Hagar and Ishmael lived, and he grew up in the wilderness.

God wants us to cry out to Him when we are afraid; He will always listen. He tells us, "Do not fear." Circumstances may seem utterly impossible, "but with God all things are possible" (Matt. 19:26).

Only One exists who can truly take away your fear. Our circumstances can create chaos, we can lose our careers, our health, even our safety net, but the tender hand of our loving God on our life will never fail!

Reflection

What are you facing today? What has you frightened? What is stealing your joy today?

Are you turning to the wrong source for comfort? Are you looking to the next job or next friend or next party to make you happy?

When difficult situations come your way, what is your typical response?

Day Four

I Am Your Shield

Do not fear, Abram,

I am a shield to you; your reward shall be very great.

Genesis 15:1

God told Abram

in a vision

not to fear ...

... because He would be a shield to him, promising Abram that his reward would be very great (Gen. 15:1). The word *shield* implies protection. The Hebrew word for shield is *māgēn*. "The basic idea of the verb is to cover over and thus shield from danger."³ The root of *māgēn* is *gānan*. Here we can gain greater insight into what God wanted to communicate to Abram. "Gānan is used only in reference to the protective guardianship of God."⁴ Specifically, in Genesis 15:1, "[m]āgēn refers to an object which provides covering and protection to the body during warfare."⁵ These two Hebrew words tell us God was reassuring Abram that He was the One who was guarding and protecting him from danger.

In our lives, fear often leads to panic. As believers, however, we don't have to panic because we know our Lord is our protector—our shield! We can trust in Him because He knows the end from the beginning. He is the One who set the stars in the heavens and placed the sun to rule by day and the moon to rule by night. Our confidence is in the One who not only created the heavens and the earth but created us—you and me. He is our protector. God is our *māgēn* and *gānan*. We can walk boldly through life knowing He will cover us when we face danger.

Marta

---

³ Robert L. Harris, Gleason L. Archer Jr., and Bruce K. Waltke, "Essay," in *Theological Wordbook of the Old Testament* (Chicago: Moody Press, 1980), 168.

⁴ Harris, Archer Jr., and Waltke, "Essay," 169.

⁵ Harris, Archer Jr., and Waltke, "Essay," 169.

Reflection

Are you relying on something other than the Lord as a means of protection?

In what ways do you try to protect yourself?

Ask the Lord to reveal Himself to you as your māgēn (shield, cover) and gānan (protective guardianship of God).

Day Five
Signs from God

Be strong and courageous! Do not tremble or be dismayed,

for the Lord your God is with you wherever you go.

Joshua 1:9

*I*n the book

of Joshua,

God appointed ...

... Joshua to take over and lead the chosen people into the Promised Land after they had wandered the wilderness forty years. What a daunting task! Most of the Israelites were terrified to cross over into the Promised Land because of the giants they had to face and conquer. Ten of the twelve leaders did not want to go. Joshua, however, along with Caleb, completely trusted in the Word of God. They knew God would protect them. In case of any doubt, God reminded them repeatedly not to be afraid.

In chapter one alone, God tells Joshua three times, "Be strong and courageous." God promises to go with them, saying, "Do not tremble or be dismayed, for the Lord your God is with you wherever you go" (Josh. 1:9). The Lord promises He will give their enemies into their hands (Josh. 8:1; 10:25). "Do not fear them . . . not one of them shall stand before you," He says in Joshua 10:8. Again in Joshua 11:6, God reminds them not to fear. It does not take a genius to find the common theme here!

God did not expect them to follow just because He said as much. He gave Israel proof—over and over. He sent plagues to the Egyptians in order to change Pharoah's heart. He allowed the Israelites to cross the Red Sea on dry land. He sent manna from heaven for them to eat. He sent a cloud by day and fire by night for them to follow. Israel had proof God would honor His Word. If He said the children of Israel should not be afraid, then they really should not be afraid!

God wants only the best for us. Remember what He has done for you in the past and "do not be afraid."

Maureen

Reflection

What proof has God given you that He loves you?

....
....
....
....
....
....
....

What are you facing today that will take courage?

....
....
....
....
....

Reflect on a promise God has given you that helps you.

....
....
....
....

Day Six
Red Sea Moments

Do not fear!

Stand by and see the salvation of the Lord

which He will accomplish for you today.

Exodus 14:13

Have you ever faced what seemed to be an impossible situation?

Perhaps you are facing one now.

As Pharaoh and his army pursued Moses and the children of Israel, God's people found themselves staring at the Red Sea and what seemed like an impossible situation. The Israelites complained, but Moses replied, "Do not fear! Stand by and see the salvation of the Lord which He will accomplish for you today; for the Egyptians whom you have seen today, you will never see them again forever. The Lord will fight for you while you keep silent" (Ex. 14:13–14).

When you face "Red Sea Moments," do you give in to fear as the Israelites did? At these moments, we have a choice: we can have either the faith of Moses or the fear of the Israelites.

Fear leads us to react in an unhealthy manner. The Israelites complained about being rescued from 400 years of oppression!

Faith is an action. Faith is moving forward with great expectation in the plan the Lord has for you while waiting for and watching the Lord fight your battle and perform a miracle.

The Lord met the Israelites in their crisis. God used the pillar of cloud, which had guided them in the desert, to lead and protect them. It served as a barricade between the Egyptian army and Israel until Moses led the people across the dry bed of the Red Sea. God had every detail perfectly orchestrated; the Israelites just needed to watch the Lord work and obey His master plan.

What was the result? Exodus 14:31 says, "When Israel saw the great power which the Lord had used against the Egyptians, the people feared the Lord, and they believed in the Lord and in His servant Moses." The children of Israel who once feared the Egyptians—man—learned to fear and revere the Lord. They also came to trust God's servant Moses.

Often God will cause us to become completely dependent on Him to reveal something greater about Himself and His character. *Marta*

Reflection

In what ways is God teaching you to be dependent on Him?

....
....
....
....
....
....
....

Are you experiencing a Red Sea Moment, or do you need a Red Sea Moment?

....
....
....
....
....

How did/do you need God to reveal Himself in your life? Journal your thoughts.

....
....
....

Day Seven
Protection

Even though I walk through the valley of the shadow of death,

I fear no evil; for Thou art with me;

Thy rod and Thy staff, they comfort me.

Psalm 23:4

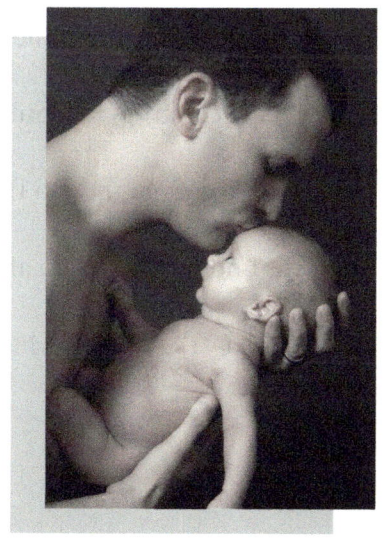

***P**salm 23 is one of the most familiar of all Scriptures.*

It is reserved for the worst of times when death looms, when sadness is overwhelming, or when we are heartbroken.

Its author, David, was a shepherd boy who became king because he was a man after God's own heart. He wrote Psalm 23 when he was at Mahanaim, wondering how the battle was going between his own forces and those of his son, Absalom. He was heartbroken over his son's rebellion, and it may have been his darkest hour.

The words in this psalm describe the trust David has in God. David writes, "The Lord is my shepherd, I shall not want. He makes me lie down in green pastures; He leads me beside quiet waters. He restores my soul; He guides me in the paths of righteousness for His name's sake. Even though I walk through the valley of the shadow of death, I fear no evil, for Thou art with me, Thy rod and Thy staff, they comfort me" (Ps. 23:1–4). He knows he is safe because God, the Great Shepherd, is with him.

David was a shepherd, so he knew what the words truly meant. The shepherd protects his flock and does what is necessary to make them stay with the rest of the flock when resting. The shepherd's rod has a point on one end and a fork on the other end. Shepherds use the point to prod the sheep along, and they place the fork over the neck of a snake when it endangers the sheep.

How many times has God needed to "prod" you along in the right direction? How often has he stopped a "snake" from causing you harm? How many times have His love and presence comforted you? You can rely on God and fear no evil in any circumstance.

Maureen

Reflection

In what way do you need comfort from the Lord today?

....
....
....
....
....
....

What experiences have you had of being protected from evil?

....
....
....
....
....

In what ways do you need to be prodded along by God to do the right thing?

....
....
....
....

Yārē'

יָרֵא

Intellectual Anticipation of Evil

The second Hebrew definition of *yārē'* is "the intellectual anticipation of evil without emphasis upon the emotional reaction."[6] My translation is "being fearful of something that might or might not happen."

---

[6] Robert L. Harris, Gleason L. Archer Jr., and Bruce K. Waltke, "Essay," in *Theological Wordbook of the Old Testament* (Chicago: Moody Press, 1980), 399.

Day Eight
Watch Your Feet

Do not be afraid of sudden fear,

nor of the onslaught of the wicked when it comes;

for the Lord will be your confidence,

and will keep your foot from being caught.

Proverbs 3:25–26

The Lord appeared to Solomon in a dream ...

... and said, "Ask what you wish Me to give you" (1 Kings 3:5). Solomon was a young king and knew he would be expected to rule a vast kingdom, so his request of the Lord was for wisdom. God did give Solomon "wisdom and very great discernment and breadth of mind" (1 Kings 4:29). Solomon, in turn, tried to pass along his wisdom to his sons, and it has come down to us in the book of Proverbs.

In Proverbs 3, Solomon tells his son to remember what he had been taught and to keep the commandments. He talks about binding kindness and goodness to his neck (v. 3) and tells him the Lord loves those he reproves (v. 12). Solomon says wisdom and discernment "will be life to your soul" (v. 22). Proverbs 3:25–26 tells us, "Do not be afraid of sudden fear, nor the onslaught of the wicked when it comes; for the Lord will be your confidence, and will keep your foot from being caught."

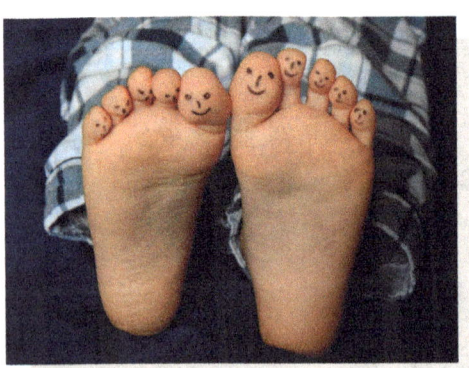

We are not told that we will never be afraid or that the wicked will never come against us. God tells us, through Solomon's words, that when fear does come, we should trust in God, and He will keep us upright.

Being fearLESS may sound like an impossibility because the human instinct in any frightening situation is to be afraid! I have learned that the only way through such circumstances is to hang on to the promise that "greater is He who is in you than he who is in the world" (I John 4:4). We may experience fear in this world, but our weapon, the Word of God, will see us through. God will protect us from the snares of life as we trust in Him.

Maureen

Reflection

Was there ever a time when you were gripped by sudden, instant fear? How did you handle it? With ongoing fear or faith?

How would you handle it differently next time?

In what ways has God kept your "foot from being caught"?

Day Nine
Fear Is a Tactic

Do not fear, for I am with you.

Isaiah 41:10

*W*e live

in an uncertain

world that seems

to be falling apart.

Yet Isaiah 41:10 teaches us, "Do not fear, for I am with you; do not anxiously look about you, for I am your God. I will strengthen you, surely I will also help you, surely I will uphold you with My righteous right hand." When the world seems to be out of control, we must remember God is sovereign. God is in complete control of everything in the entire universe.

Yet when we hear of one calamity after another, we often succumb to fear. Fear is a tactic of the evil one. It can immobilize us. Fear can stop us from accomplishing God's assignments for our lives. When life seems to spiral out of control, we must not only know God's Word, but His Word must also be so embedded in our minds and hearts that the only fear we have is a reverential fear of the Lord.

Fear was prevalent in Isaiah's time too. The Hebrew word for fear, *yārē'*, appears twenty-seven times in the book of Isaiah. His message to Israel often encouraged them not to fear, no matter the circumstances in which they found themselves.

Considering the chaos that seems so prevalent today, we must trust in God's sovereignty, even when we don't understand. The return of Christ is near. We must focus on His plan and purpose, which is to pray for the salvation of the lost and to speak His truth to the nations. This is not a task for the timid and fearful, but it is *our* calling. We are called to be FearLESS.

Marta

Reflection

Are you spending time with the Lord daily?

....

....

....

....

....

....

What is your favorite verse? How has it changed your life?

....

....

....

....

....

Do you have a list of people for whom you are praying for salvation? If not, why not start one today?

....

....

....

....

....

Day Ten

Treasures

Be at ease, do not be afraid. Your God and the God of your father has given you treasure in your sacks.

Genesis 43:23

*J*oseph was sold into slavery by his brothers ...

... who were jealous of him, but he honored God throughout his life and was rewarded with a good position and wealth. During a great famine, his brothers came to buy food from Joseph (unaware he was their brother). By rights, he should have loathed them and treated them badly, but he loved them because they were his family. This was their second trip to see Joseph, and he was overjoyed to see them. They had visited before to purchase food and found all their money returned to them after they had journeyed home. On their second trip, they brought the original money and additional funds to purchase more food. They were afraid they would be mistaken for thieves and become slaves because their original money was found on them.

As they tried to explain what had happened, Joseph's steward told them, "Be at ease, do not be afraid. Your God and the God of your father has given you treasure in your sacks" (Gen. 43:23). Joseph had returned the money when they were unaware. He did not want them to be afraid of

what might happen to them.

It is much the same with each of us. God tells us not to be afraid. He continually fills our "sacks" with riches, even when we fail Him repeatedly. He is a God of love and wants His children to be

happy. He longs to celebrate with us as Joseph did with his brothers. We need only turn to Him when we have sinned, and He will forgive us. He is our Father and is always overjoyed when we go to Him. He loves us.

Some of the riches in my sack are beautiful sunsets, a wonderful family to love, books to read, eyes to see with, and air to breathe.

Maureen

Reflection

List some of the "riches in your sack."

....
....
....
....
....

How can you use these gifts to bless others?

....
....
....
....
....

Journal a time when the Lord blessed you.

....
....
....
....
....

Day Eleven
Confident

Though a host encamp against me,

my heart will not fear; Though war arise against me,

in spite of this I shall be confident.

Psalm 27:3

Have you ever felt

as if an enemy

were out

to get you...

... or as if obstacles arise at every turn?

David was a man well acquainted with obstacles and often chased by enemies. He was anointed king while still a youth tending his father's sheep, but he spent years in service to King Saul, the one whom David was ordained by God to replace one day. David's fame rose while Saul was still king. As a result, King Saul became jealous and devised endless failed plots to assassinate David.

Theologians believe David wrote Psalm 27 shortly after Saul's first murderous attempt sent him into hiding in caves. David cries out, "Though a host encamp against me, my heart will not fear; Though war arise against me, in spite of this I shall be confident" (v. 3).

Why could David be so confident? He says, "The Lord is my light and my salvation; whom should I fear? The Lord is the defense of my life; whom should I dread?" (Psalm 27:1). He understood God would be the one to defeat his enemies (v. 2). All David asked was that the Lord allow him to dwell in His house all his days (v. 4). David's relationship with the Lord was more important to him than his life. He knew if he sought the Lord first, the Lord would look after his life (v. 5).

In the final verse of this psalm, David says, "Wait for the Lord" (v. 14). This is a reminder to himself and to us. No enemy could change or alter God's ordained path for David's life. David knew one day he would be king. Why? Because the Lord said so. Though a host of enemies encamp around you, don't fear, but walk boldly forward, confident in the plans the Lord has in store for you.

Maureen

Reflection

David's life was ordained by God; do you believe yours is as well?

What plans do you believe the Lord has in store for you?

Are you waiting in faith and confidence for God's purposes to be revealed in your life?

....
....
....
....
....
....
....
....
....
....
....
....
....
....
....
....

Day Twelve
Call on the Lord

Thou didst draw near when I called on Thee;

Thou didst say, "Do not fear!"

Lamentations 3:57

*F**ear comes*

in many ways...

… and often makes a difficult season even worse. I have been in fear and dread of the one-year anniversary of the passing of one of my dearest and closest friends. I was afraid the day would send me into a very sad place, and I did not want to go there.

This friend knew me. She knew the good, the bad, and the ugly. She knew me with all my faults and failures. She knew how to make me laugh, and she thought I was funny! Sometimes we would be together only once every six months, but we never felt any awkwardness, never even a moment's hesitation when we picked up where we had left off. She could stay in my home and be very comfortable in my world. My friend was with me through some tough life events and some wonderful ones, and she loved me with an unfailing love.

I reminded myself Jesus is better than any earthly best friend. God knows me even better and loves me even more! He knows *all* my faults and failures. He does not get mad at me if I don't "hang out" with Him but welcomes me with open arms the minute I reach out. He is always comfortable in my home. Overwhelming sadness was not going to happen as long as I looked to the

God who knit me in the womb and tells me 365 times in the Bible not to be afraid.

As believers in Jesus, we have a "friend who sticks closer than a brother" (Prov. 18:24). We only have to call on Him and be reminded of His words in Lamentations: "Thou didst draw near when I called on Thee; Thou didst say, 'Do not fear!'"

Maureen

Reflection

Write down a time when your fear of something proved to be unfounded.

....
....
....
....
....
....

What did you learn from this test?

....
....
....
....
....

What could you have done to draw near to the Lord?

....
....
....
....

Yārē'

יָרֵא

Reverence or Awe

The *Theological Wordbook of the Old Testament* calls this meaning of fear "the God-fearer."

The most frequent usage of the substantive is to refer to the "God-fearer" (different names or expressions for God may be used). Clearly, substantival examples which show fear as an emotion (1 above) or as an anticipation of evil (2 above) are found (e.g. Ex. 9:20; Deut. 20:8; Judg. 7:3). More frequently, the emphasis is upon awe or reverence rather than terror (Ps. 112:1; Eccl. 8:12).

The "God-fearer" will implement his fear in practical righteousness or piety. Job, as a God-fearer, avoids evil (Job 1:1). In Psalm 128:1, the "fearer" of the Lord walks in his ways. The fearers of the Lord may be those whose particular piety is evidenced by a response to God's message. The "fearer" of God is contrasted with the wicked (Eccl. 8:13). It is desired that office holders be fearers of God (Neh. 7:2). Blessings are provided for fearers of God:

- happiness (i.e., "blessed"; Ps. 112:1)

- goodness from God (Ps. 31:19)

- provision of needs (Ps. 34:9)

- protection (Ps. 33:18–19)

- overshadowing mercy (i.e., *ḥesed*; Ps. 103:11)

- and promise of fulfilled desires (Ps. 145:19).[7]

---

[7] A. Bowling, "907 יָרֵא," in *Theological Wordbook of the Old Testament*, electronic edition, ed. R. L. Harris, G. L. Archer Jr., and B. K. Waltke (Chicago: Moody Press, 1999), 400.

Heavenly Father vs. Earthly Father

My Story

In 1998, I joined the missionary staff of a church-planting organization known today as e3Partners. Within weeks of being there, I met with the marketing manager, who discovered my background in marketing and advertising. He suggested I begin working with him instead of the church-planting team.

I woke up the next morning contemplating the conversation. As I opened God's Word, He clearly spoke to my heart. I will never forget what I heard. God speaks in a still, small voice, yet to me it sounded like a trumpet. He said, *If you will stop trying to please your earthly father and start trying to please your heavenly Father, I will do great and mighty things in and through your life.*

You see, after the marketing meeting, I knew my father would be very proud of my taking on this marketing role. Approval and acceptance is something every child wants from his or her parents. I had come to a crossroads. Was I going to please my heavenly Father or my earthly father? The choice was mine. The next business day, I walked into the marketing manager's office and declined his generous offer.

There were no fireworks, and no one really knew the significance of my choice. But choosing God over man was a defining moment in my life. The world may never think my life as great and mighty, but God's ways are not man's ways. I have never looked back from that "God-fearer" Day.

Marta

Day Thirteen
This Is Only a Test

*Do not stretch out your hand against the lad,
and do nothing to him; for now I know that you fear God,
since you have not withheld your son, your only son, from Me.*

Genesis 22:12

God tested Abraham by ordering him to offer his long-promised son as a burnt offering.

This was the son born when Abraham was one hundred years old, the son God promised whose descendants would be as numerous as the stars in the heavens.

Let's understand, God did not intend Abraham's son to be sacrificed. This is why it was a test. Abraham believed if he followed through with the sacrifice, God would raise Isaac from the dead. Hebrews 11:19 explains, "Abraham considered that God is able to raise men even from the dead; from which he also received him back as a type."

Abraham could not know the outcome of the Lord's command, but he was obedient. Genesis 22 tells us Abraham took his son, wood, and a knife, saying, "We will worship and return to you." (v. 5).

Isaac questioned his father: "Where is the lamb for the burnt offering?" (v. 7).

Abraham replied, "God will provide for Himself the lamb for the burnt offering, my son." (v. 12).

Abraham raised the knife, and the angel of the Lord stopped him. "Do not stretch out your hand against the lad, and do nothing to him; for now I know that you fear God, since you have not withheld your son, your only son, from Me."

Abraham's fear of the Lord led to his obedience, which allowed Abraham to know and understand God in a new way. Abraham called the place *Jehovah-jireh*, which means "the Lord will provide." Abraham learned God would provide in his most difficult moments.

God wants you to know Him as your Jehovah-jireh. He wants to be your provider. Our responsibility is to obey Him in our most difficult situations and watch Him work miraculously in our lives.

Marta

Reflection

How are you being tested today?

....
....
....
....
....
....

What do you need the Lord to provide?

....
....
....
....
....
....

What is God calling you to lay on His altar?

....
....
....
....
....
....

Day Fourteen
Wisdom

If you will fear the Lord and serve Him, and listen to His voice

and not rebel against the command of the Lord,

then both you and also the king who reigns over you

will follow the Lord your God.

1 Samuel 12:14

Samuel was the fifteenth and final judge of Israel.

He was honest and fair, impartially following God's law. He was also a prophet who convinced Israel to turn from their wicked ways and return to the Lord with all their hearts. The Israelites were to serve Him alone, remove all idols, fast, and pray to the Lord, and they would be victorious against the Philistines.

Israel obeyed the Lord and was triumphant. In 1 Samuel 7:12, Samuel placed a rock at the place where Ebenezer had won the battle, telling the people, "Thus far the Lord has helped us."

The people of Israel seemed to have forgotten all the "thus fars" the Lord had done for them.

They cried out for a king. All the neighboring regions had kings, and they wanted to be like everyone else. The Lord told Samuel not to be disheartened by this request. The people were rebelling against God, not against Samuel. Saul was the first appointed king, and in 1 Samuel 12:14, Samuel tells the people, "If you will fear the Lord and serve Him, and listen to His voice and not rebel against the command of the Lord, then both you and also the king who reigns over you will follow the Lord your God."

The "thus fars" in my life are too numerous to count. Thus far I have a roof over my head. Thus far I have food to eat daily. Thus far I have good health. Thus far I am able to attend church and praise the Lord publicly.

In Proverbs 9:10, King Solomon declares, "The fear of the Lord is the beginning of wisdom." Reverence and awe of God are the "fear" of which he speaks. Instead of searching for something to guard us against earthly fears, we need a healthy fear of the Lord!

Maureen

Reflection

Write down three "thus fars" God has given you.

....
....
....
....
....

How did these bring you closer to fearing the Lord?

....
....
....
....
....

What does a healthy fear of the Lord look like?

....
....

Yārē'

Righteous Behavior, or Piety

In several passages, "fearing" and proper living are so closely related as to be virtually synonymous ideas (Lev. 19:14; 25:17; 2 Kings 17:34; Deut. 17:19). It is plausible that this usage of "to fear" as a virtual synonym for righteous living or piety grew out of viewing "fear"—in any of the senses above—as the motivation which produced righteous living. This practical, active fear is the kind of fear for which God rewarded the Egyptian midwives (Ex. 1:17, 21). This kind of fear was most appropriately learned by reading the Law (Deut. 31:11–12). One righteous deed repeatedly and emphatically associated with "fearing" God is kindness to the stranger or resident alien (e.g., Deut. 10:18–20; 25:18).[8]

---

[8] A. Bowling, "907 יָרֵא." in *Theological Wordbook of the Old Testament,* electronic edition, ed. R. L. Harris, G. L. Archer Jr., and B. K. Waltke (Chicago: Moody Press, 1999), 400.

Day Fifteen
Midwives

So God was good to the midwives,

and the people multiplied, and became very mighty.

And it came about because the midwives feared

God, that He established households for them.

Exodus 1:20–21

The pharaoh of Egypt commanded the Israelite midwives...

… to kill the male Hebrew children at birth but allow the females to live. The motivations behind the order were fear and the desire to control. Pharaoh

feared the people would multiply greatly and overtake the Egyptians. He tried to control the people by first appointing taskmasters to oppress them with hard labor. When they continued to multiply and flourish, Pharaoh sent an edict to kill the baby boys.

Scripture tells us the midwives defied the king's order. Not only did they defy the order, they lied to the king. Why? Because they feared the Lord.

When man's laws are contradictory to God's laws, the answer is clear: we must obey God rather than man. How did God feel about the midwives' lies and deception? Exodus 1:20–21 teaches us, "So God was good to the midwives, and the people multiplied, and became very mighty. And it came about because the midwives feared God, that He established households for them."

God blessed the midwives because of their fear of Him. When we are placed in a difficult position and must choose between God and man, we must be like the midwives and trust in God to honor our decisions to serve Him. We must understand our King is a heavenly King, and He is our Creator and Sustainer. He is the giver of our life.

　　We must not live in fear of the created, for they too had the same breath of life breathed into their body to make them a living soul. As the divide deepens between man's laws and God's laws, we must choose to stand for truth. Fearing God and trusting Him, we know our decisions will find favor with God as we continue to choose Him over the world.

Reflection

Has there been a time when conflict arose in your life because you obeyed God instead of man?

In what ways are you seeing man's laws coming into contradiction with God's laws?

On whose side will you stand?

Day Sixteen
911 Prayers

For all of them were trying to frighten us, thinking,

"They will become discouraged with the work

and it will not be done."

But now, O God, strengthen my hands.

Nehemiah 6:9

Sanballat, Tobiah, and Geshem were enemies of Nehemiah.

They continually mocked and ridiculed him in an attempt to discourage him from his God-given task of rebuilding the wall in Jerusalem. Sanballat sent a letter to Nehemiah inviting him to a meeting. Nehemiah, understanding their true motive was to harm him, remained steadfast in continuing his work.

After five more attempts with the same results, Sanballat slandered Nehemiah's character. Nehemiah 6:9 gives us his response: "For all of them were trying to frighten us, thinking, 'They will become discouraged with the work and it will not be done.' But now, O God, strengthen my hands."

Fear is a tactic of the evil one to stop God's people from accomplishing our God-given work. Did you notice how Nehemiah handled the situation? He prayed what I call a "911 prayer"—you know, the ones said in a panic or an emergency. A 911 prayer is when you don't have time for lengthy eloquence. You need an answer now! So you cry out with a one-sentence prayer—a prayer of desperation.

Nehemiah knew the cost of not finishing his assignment. The wall was a source of protection — a first line of defense for the city. He also knew the spiritual attacks that had been increasing in severity were not going to stop. Nehemiah's formula to overcome fear was to pray for the Lord to strengthen him to continue the work.

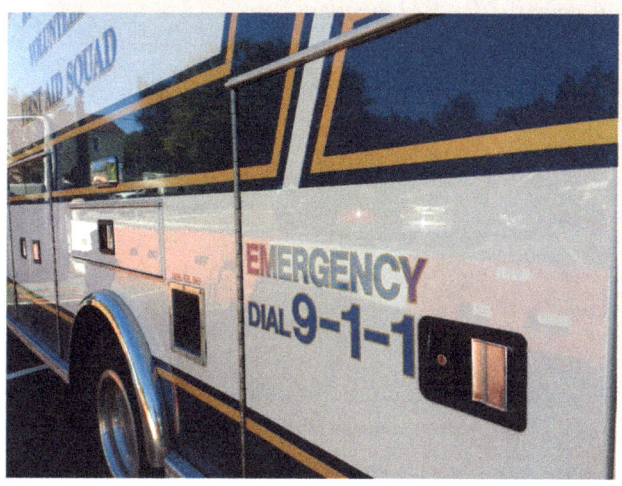

Have you felt like Nehemiah, knowing your job is impossible without the Lord's protection and strength? You wake up every day to another challenge and obstacle. The enemy's relentless attacks keep trying to paralyze you. Learn from Nehemiah: pray 911 prayers and keep progressing in the plans and purpose God has for your life.

Marta

Reflection

Have you ever said a 911 prayer?

How did God show up?

When you pray a 911 prayer, should you stop doing what God has asked you to do and wait for the answer, or should you keep working?

Day Seventeen
Correction Equals Change

Lift up your face . . .

and you would be steadfast and not fear.

Job 11:15

T he book of Job

in the Old Testament

is one of great pain...

... and amazing restoration. I look upon chapter eleven as a test of Job's foundation — the foundation he had built upon our Lord. It makes me take a close look at my own foundation. Even in the most fearful moments, Job never wavered. Even when his friends went against him, his foundation never shook. Even when his wife told him to curse the Lord, Job was steady. The Lord allowed Satan to take everything away from Job—his home, children, livestock, servants. He attacked Job's health, covering him in painful sores. I sincerely pray I would be strong enough to remain faithful in the midst of such severe suffering.

In Job 5:21, his "friend" Eliphaz, who is convinced that Job has done something terribly wrong to warrant this type of pain from God, tells him, "Neither will you be afraid of violence when it comes." He is referring to one who accepts correction from God and does not falter. Later in the book of Job, his "friend" Zophar, also convinced that Job's sin is the source of his pain, tells him that if he puts aside sin, then he will "lift up [his] face . . . and . . . be steadfast and not fear" (Job 11:15).

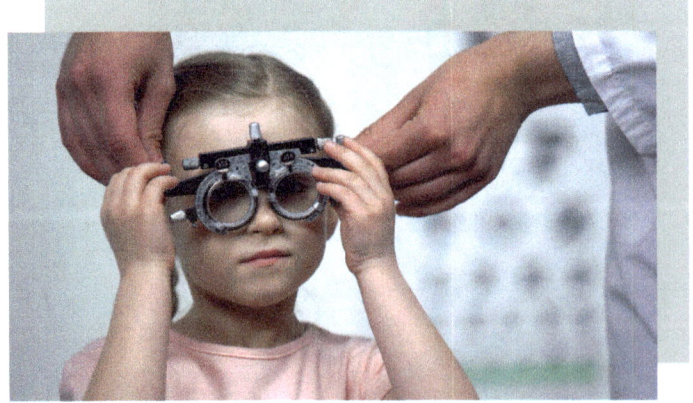

Correction is not usually something we like but often what we need in order to change our behavior. Suffering can be productive when we are truly ready to learn from a trustworthy God. God knew that Job would not succumb to

Satan and also that Job's wife needed to learn the strength of Job's character. Job had a conversation with God and knew for certain that it was God who was in charge. God restored Job's losses many times over—a reward for standing firm on the foundation of the Lord. It is time to stand, lift up your face to the Lord, and be FearLESS!

Maureen

Reflection

On a scale of 1–10, with 10 being the highest, how firm is your foundation with the Lord?

What events lead to the success or failure of your foundation?

What is your plan to strengthen it?

Yārē'

יָרֵא

Formal Religious Worship

The clearest example of "fearing" as formal religious worship occurs in describing the religious syncretists of the Northern Kingdom who "feared" the Lord in respect to cultic worship (2 Kings 17:32–34) while not "fearing" the Lord in respect to righteous obedience to his law. The formal cultic elements mentioned in Deuteronomy 14:22–23 suggest that this is the kind of fear to be learned in that context. In light of the above discussion and of the context of Joshua 22, the RSV is probably correct in translating "fear" as "worship" there (v. 25).

There are a few passages in which "fearing" seems to mean "being a devotee or follower." This usage could reflect either usages 4 or 5 above. Related substantival examples will be discussed below under *yārē'*, but possible verbal examples are found in Job 1:9 and II Chronicles 6:33. [9]

---

[9] A. Bowling, "907 יָרֵא." in *Theological Wordbook of the Old Testament*, electronic edition, ed. R. L. Harris, G. L. Archer Jr., and B. K. Waltke (Chicago: Moody Press, 1999), 400.

Day Eighteen
Battle Cry

Do not be afraid of them;

remember the Lord who is great and awesome, and fight for your

brothers, your sons, your daughters,

your wives, and your houses.

Nehemiah 4:14

Yārē', the Hebrew word for fear ...

... is used over 382 times in the Old Testament. The *Theological Wordbook of the Old Testament* teaches us there are five uses for this word. The most obvious one is emotional fear. Second is the intellectual anticipation of evil. The third use is about the "fear of the Lord." This meaning of *yārē'* implies a reverence or awe for who God is. The fourth meaning is righteous behavior or piety. Our behavior is a reflection of this belief because of our reverence for who God is.

But the final meaning surprises me the most. It is formal religious worship.

Nehemiah 4:14 says, "When I saw their fear, I rose and spoke to the nobles, the officials and the rest of the people: 'Do not be afraid of them; remember the Lord who is great and awesome and fight for your brothers, your sons, your daughters, your wives, and your houses.'" The word *awesome* in this verse is the word *yārē'*.

Nehemiah was teaching the children of Israel that when they experienced emotional fear, their response should be to remember the Lord is great and awesome—*yārē'*. Therefore, because He is *yārē'*, we can worship Him!

Nehemiah wanted to show the strength of the people, so he gave them a battle cry. In Nehemiah 4:20, he commands, "At whatever place you hear the sound of the trumpet, rally to us there. Our God will fight for us."

We can learn how to battle our emotional fears. When we are afraid, we can confidently worship the Lord, knowing He will fight for us. *Marta*

Reflection

What is your normal response when you are afraid?

How is the Lord equipping you to fight?

What are some ways we can express our reverence or awe for who God is?

Yir'a

יִרְאָה

The Hebrew word *yir'a* is used forty-three times in the Old Testament. *Yir'a* is used both as a noun and as the infinitive for *yārē'*. *Yārē'* is found in all usages except for formal religious worship.

The usages of this noun are similar to those of the verb. It may refer to the emotion of terror or fear (Ps. 55:5 [H 6]; Ezek. 30:13). This terror may be put into men's hearts by God (Ex. 20:20; Deut. 2:25). Isaiah 7:25 uses the term for an unemotional anticipation of evil. When God is the object of fear, the emphasis is again upon awe or reverence. This attitude of reverence is the basis for real wisdom (Job 28:28; Ps. 111:10; Prov. 9:10; 15:33). Indeed, the phrase sets the theme for the book of Proverbs. It is used in 1:7 and recurs in 9:10 and twelve other verses.

The fear of the Lord

    is to hate evil (8:13)

        is a fountain of life (14:27)

            it tendeth to life (19:23)

                prolongeth days (10:27)

Numerous passages relate this fear of God to piety and righteous living — it motivates faithful living (Jer. 32:40). Fear of God results in caring for strangers (Gen. 20:11). Just rule is rule in the fear of God (2 Sam. 23:3). Fear of the Almighty does not withhold kindness from friends (Job 6:14). Economic abuses against fellow Jews were contrary to the fear of God (Neh. 5:9). The fear of the Lord turns men from evil (Prov. 16:6). [10]

Yir'a leaves the reader understanding God is all powerful. He is El Shaddai, God Almighty.

---

[10] A. Bowling, "907 יָרֵא." in *Theological Wordbook of the Old Testament*, electronic edition, ed. R. L. Harris, G. L. Archer Jr., and B. K. Waltke (Chicago: Moody Press, 1999), 401.

Day Nineteen
Fear God, Not Man

I did not do so because of the fear of God.

Nehemiah 5:15

Nehemiah heard the nobles and rulers of Israel were practicing usury ...

... with the remnant in Jerusalem and became very angry. Usury is the practice of lending money at unreasonably high interest rates. The leaders were getting rich while the  laymen were stuck in bondage. Nehemiah condemned the leaders because the children of Israel had been rescued from bondage and were treating their own people just like the nations who had enslaved them.

In Nehemiah 5:9, he tells the nobles, "The thing which you are doing is not good; should you not walk in the fear of our God because of the reproach of the nations, our enemies?"

Nehemiah's fear of the Lord was more important to him than money, relationships, or community standing. Nehemiah chose to honor God in his leadership role. He chose *not* to take the governor's food allowance and *not* to put a burden on the people. Why? Because Nehemiah feared God, not man.

Nehemiah was one man going against many. He could have chosen to remain silent but stood up for those who were being taken advantage of. Nehemiah could not in good conscience go against God's principles in the treatment of others. He practiced what Leviticus 19:18 said, "Love your neighbor as yourself." Charging God's people usury was in direct contradiction of God's laws.

We as believers are called by God to be set apart from unbelievers in how we treat others. How you as a Christian leader treat those whom you lead teaches others about your relationship with God. You have a choice. Will you be like Nehemiah? Will your relationships with others reflect your relationship with the Lord? Whom will you fear, God or man? *Marta*

Reflection

Do you see unhealthy worldly practices in biblical leaders today? If so, what did you learn from Nehemiah to effect change?

....
....
....
....
....
....
....

What would fearing God look like today?

....
....
....
....
....
....

Do people recognize you as a believer by the way you treat others? If not, what changes do you need to make?

....
....
....

Day Twenty

Fear of the Lord

The fear of the Lord is the beginning of wisdom;

A good understanding have all those who do His commandments;

His praise endures forever.

Psalm 111:10

What does it mean to fear the Lord?

It means a reverence or awe of God, but what does it mean to live that out in our daily lives? Psalm 111:10 teaches, "The fear of the Lord is the beginning of wisdom; A good understanding have all those who do His commandments; His praise endures forever." In other words, those who obey the Lord's commandments fear the Lord. How simple!

Proverbs 29:25 tells us, "The fear of man brings a snare." Fearing man is in stark contrast to fearing God. We are entrapped when consumed with people pleasing rather than God pleasing. I was once a people pleaser, and I have to tell you, it's exhausting! Now I consider myself a recovering people pleaser. Today, my heart's desire is to please God and to be a "yes woman" for Jesus and Jesus alone.

Peter and John were released after being flogged and imprisoned. They were warned by the Sanhedrin to quit testifying about Jesus. Brought back before the council, they face the high priest's rebuke: "We gave you strict orders not to continue teaching in this name, and behold, you have filled Jerusalem with your teaching, and intend to bring this man's blood upon us" (Acts 5:28). Peter and John's response is simple: "We must obey God rather than men" (Acts 5:29).

We often try to find a secret formula for living a successful Christian life. The reality is simple — obey God. A favorite saying of mine is "Obedience always equals blessings." We are personally blessed when we fear and obey the Lord, and others are also blessed. Who are you going to choose to please today?

Reflection

Has the fear of man been a snare in your life?

How is God teaching you to be a God pleaser instead of a people pleaser?

How has your obedience led to blessing others?

Day Twenty One
Fools Hate Knowledge

Then they will call on me, but I will not answer;
they will seek me diligently, but they will not find me,
because they hated knowledge,
and did not choose the fear of the Lord.

Proverbs 1:28–29

In our culture,

we serve ourselves,

the created, instead of

serving our Creator.

We take credit for our talents that were given by God instead of honoring the One who imparted them to us.

It doesn't matter if we are gifted at sports, music, art, science, or finances. God has given us our talents to cultivate and use for His glory. These are blessings the Lord has bestowed upon us.

Yet when it comes to giving glory to self, there is a darker side. Today we see the prevalence of sexual sins such as adultery, fornication, homosexuality, and transgenderism as well as lust for power and control. Romans 1:24–25 says, "God gave them over in the lusts of their hearts . . . For they exchanged the truth of God for a lie, and worshiped and served the creature rather than the Creator."

God's Word teaches in Proverbs 1:29, "They hated knowledge and did not choose the fear of the Lord." How do you find God's knowledge? You find it in His Word, of course. God's Word offers everything we need to live our lives. His Word corrects us and trains us in righteousness. Daily investing in seeking knowledge from the Lord will keep us from sitting at the feet of the foolish who scoff at God.

Proverbs 1:29 tells us to choose the fear of the Lord. This tells us we must make a conscious decision to choose God's principles and precepts instead of man's. Often this brings us into direct conflict with the modern world.

Reflection

What do you know God wants you to do?

....
....
....
....
....
....

Is there a possibility it will bring conflict or be unpopular?

....
....
....
....
....
....

Is it your nature to give credit to self or to God? What changes do you need to make?

....
....
....
....
....

Bālah

בָּלַה

בָּלַה (bālah) trouble. "Occurs only in the Piel (Ez. 4:4)" [11] Ezra 4:4 is the only time this Hebrew word appears in the Old Testament. In English, we have different tenses such as present, past, and future. Hebrew also has tenses, and piel is one form. "A verb in the piel system typically infers a causative meaning." [12]

With Ezra 4:4 as our example, "Then the people of the land discouraged the people of Judah, and frightened them from building." This would tell us the verb is *frightened* and the subject of the verb is *the people of the land*; therefore, the people of the land are making the children of Israel frightened. The children of Israel are fearing man and not God. Nor are they trusting in the Lord to take care of them when they are on assignment for the Living God.

---

[11] Robert L. Harris, Gleason L. Archer Jr., & Bruce K. Waltke, eds., *Theological Wordbook of the Old Testament*, electronic ed. (Chicago: Moody Press, 1999), 111.

[12] "The Hebrew Piel Verbal Stem: Intensifying The Idea." *RDRD Bible Study*, Dec. 20, 2019, rdrdbiblestudy.com/the-hebrew-piel-verbal-stem-intensifying-the-idea/.

Romanian Train Station

My Story

In 2002, while my husband and I were living as missionaries in Romania, a small team from America arrived to help for a few weeks. We were in the city of Constanta for the day, where we had been invited to assist another ministry working with street children. My husband and I were familiar with street children, but the ones we worked with on a daily basis were very different from the ones we were going to meet that night. These children lived in the train station and were "city" street children. This meant most likely they sniffed glue and other harmful chemicals to subdue their hunger, making their behavior erratic and emotional.

We met at the appointed time to receive our instructions. It was evening, and we were told to walk through the tunnel toward the light. We needed to go single file, holding hands or placing one hand on another's shoulder.

My husband and I decided I would lead the group, setting the pace, and he would be the rear guard. As we entered the tunnel, it was alarming how dark it had become. It was not possible to see anything except the tiny light in the distance. About halfway through the tunnel, I began to feel hands touching me. And they weren't from our team members in our single-file line.

Fear gripping my insides, I wondered what I should do. If I showed fear, I knew the entire team would become fearful. These unpredictable, chemically altered children could do anything, and we were helpless. I could ask everyone to turn around, or we could trust in the Lord who had brought us this far and walk toward the tiny light.

After what seemed like an hour but was probably only five minutes, we arrived at the end of the tunnel. There, about one hundred children and youth greeted us. The oldest was around twenty-one, but because of the glue sniffing, they all acted about eight.

What started out as a frightening experience turned into a sweet time of fellowship and ministry. We fed the children sandwiches and water, for which they were very grateful, taught them songs about Jesus, and played a few games. Finally, we gave a short but powerful gospel presentation.

God was glorified as we ministered to the "least of these." That night, He opened our eyes to the children who needed Him most.

I'll never forget my Romanian experiences when God showed me how to love those most people considered unlovable. The sharing of God's love usually starts with us stepping outside our comfort zones and opening our eyes to see what God has in store for our lives.

Day Twenty Two

Recognize the Fiery Darts

Then the people of the land discouraged the people of Judah, and frightened them from building.

Ezra 4:4

The enemy has been using the same strategies throughout history.

To overcome, we must recognize his fiery darts. Through God's Word, I have discerned the first tactics of the enemy are manipulation and fear.

God stirred the heart of King Cyrus of Persia to rebuild the temple in Jerusalem. After the foundation was laid, Judah's enemies attempted to manipulate Zerubbabel, saying, "Let us build with you, for we, like you, seek your God; and we have been sacrificing to Him since the days of Esarhaddon king of Assyria, who brought us up here" (Ezra 4:2).

Zerubbabel rightfully denied this request. Ezra 4:4 tells us, "Then the people of the land discouraged the people of Judah, and frightened them from building." Sadly, this tactic was so successful, the project to rebuild the temple was delayed fourteen years.

If only Zerubbabel and the children of Israel had learned from their history! Both Moses and David understood God was the One who would fight their battles and shatter their enemies. After the children of Israel crossed the Red Sea, they sang, "Thy right hand, O Lord, is majestic in

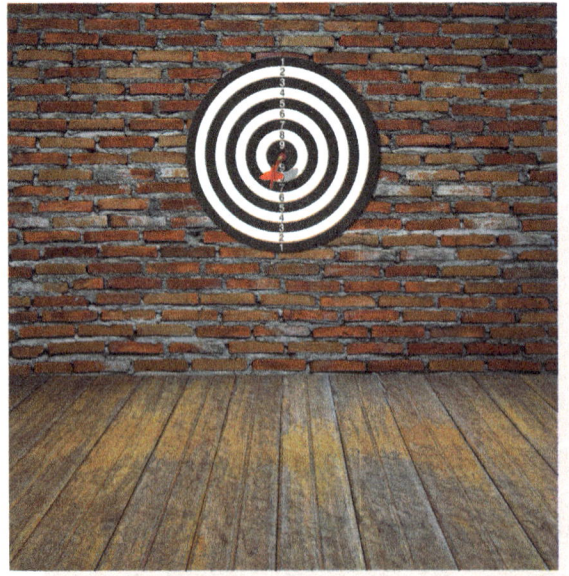

power, Thy right hand, O Lord, shatters the enemy" (Ex. 15:6). King David said of King Saul, "The Lord delivered me from my strong enemy, And from those who hated me, for they were too mighty for me" (Ps. 18:17).

Fourteen years later when the rebuilding began, the enemy once more used his familiar tactics of fear and intimidation. But the people had learned from their failures, and God's temple was finally completed.

We too must not allow fear to stop the work of the Lord. Walk forward and trust the Lord to shatter your enemies. —Marta

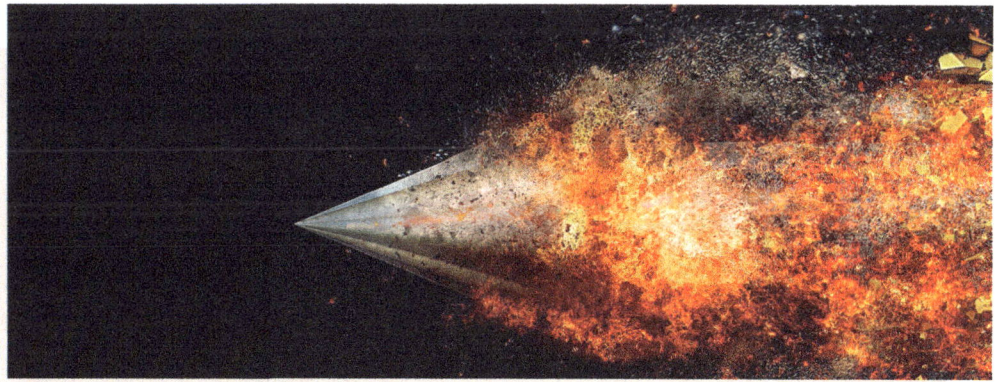

Reflection

Is there a work to which you sense the Lord is calling you?

What is your plan to fight the manipulation and fear of the enemy?

How are you starting to recognize the fiery darts of the enemy?

Měgôrâ

מְגוֹרָה

This root means to be intimidated before a stronger or superior being or thing. It is used of fear toward men, animals, and God. The Moabites feared the Israelites when the Moabites appeared on the horizon because of their great numbers (Num. 22:3).

Judges are instructed not to fear man, i.e., not to let the social position of any adversary in litigation intimidate them nor sway them in judgment (Deut 1:17).

The threats of a false prophet were not to turn the people from God (Deut. 18:22).

Although David was only a stripling, the gifts bestowed on him impressed and then frightened Saul (1 Sam. 18:15).

Job rejects the implied charge of secret sin, avowing his innocency and claiming that he would see God in the flesh; therefore his slanderers should fear judgment (Job 19:29).

Leviahan strikes fear in even the mighty men of the earth (Job 41:25).

The Lord is pictured as fearing the boasters of the heathen if they chasten Israel (Deut. 32:27).

But Samaria is to fear the consequences of the idols in Bethel (Hos. 10:5). [13]

---

[13] H. G. Stigers, "332 גור." in *Theological Wordbook of the Old Testament*, electronic edition, ed. R. L. Harris, G. L. Archer Jr., and B. K. Waltke (Chicago: Moody Press, 1999), 157.

My New BFF

Our Story

Maureen moved to Texas in 2011 and was looking for a location to teach a Bible-based program called Just Moved to women who had relocated to the area for their husband's work.

Prestonwood Baptist Church was the perfect location for the class. The pastor was in favor of Maureen teaching it on the morning of the regularly scheduled women's Bible study, with one stipulation. A resident church Bible teacher needed to be in the class at all times.

You guessed it! Marta was assigned to be the "resident teacher." This was a new experience for both Marta and Maureen. Marta had never been a resident teacher in a class someone else was teaching, and Maureen was not used to having what she considered a "boss" looking over her shoulder all through the class.

Marta was nervous because the pastor wanted to make sure this worked well. She bought a new outfit to make sure she "looked" the part. She was also nervous to meet this woman for whom her pastor had rolled out the red carpet. Maureen, meanwhile, was worried that this "resident teacher" would find her unfit to teach the class. It all began with two women apprehensively saying yes to God, who placed them in that same classroom to teach about Him.

Looking back ten years later, we can't help but see the hand of God all over this situation. Marta and Maureen have traveled halfway around the world on missions for God. Maureen served on Marta's editing team for two of her three Bible studies. In 2019, Marta and Maureen became cohosts of the *Under God* radio program on GraceAndTruthRadio.World. Maureen is also on the board of directors for Marta's ministry, Words of Grace & Truth. And now Marta and Maureen have cowritten this devotional.

None of these things would have happened if we both had not fully trusted God's plan and walked together through every door He opened for us.

Maureen

Marta

Day Twenty Three

Faith or Fear

I sought the Lord, and He answered me,

and delivered me from all my fears.

Psalm 34:4

*D**avid was in*

hiding

from King Saul...

... who wanted to kill him. He chose to flee into the land of Gath ruled by King Achish, thinking he would be safe there. However, his fame had preceded him. The giant Goliath he had slain was from Gath, and the people were singing in the streets, "Saul has slain thousands, And David his tens of thousands" (1 Sam. 18:7).

David prayed earnestly but silently because he was among the servants of Gath, and God took away his fears. He feigned madness and was set free from the king of Gath. In Psalm 34:4, David says, "I sought the Lord, and He answered me, And delivered me from all my fears." He is describing his actions of turning away from sin and returning to the Lord in total faith that God would take care of him as long as he walked with the Lord. David was fearful until he turned back to God for direction.

We can have fear about so many things — some of it justified but much because we have not truly given our lives to the Lord and let Him take charge of us. The opposite of fear is not hope, strength, or courage but faith.

The first thing God wants us to do when fear starts creeping in is to repent and turn back to Him. This will only happen when we confess our sins and make Jesus our primary focus. It does *not* mean we will be delivered from all our earthly problems but that God will take away our fears. He will deliver us as he did David.

Maureen

Reflection

Reflect on a time of trouble when you did not seek the Lord. What was the outcome?

....
....
....
....
....
....

How would you do it differently today?

....
....
....
....
....

What advice would you give a friend to help them seek God?

....
....
....
....
....

Day Twenty Four

Deliverer

I sought the Lord, and He answered me,

And delivered me from all my fears.

Psalm 34:4

Because we live in uncertain times, fear is prevalent.

Some days, fear can surround and engulf us. It can manifest and disguise itself as uncertainty, anger, insomnia, or anxiety. Psalm 34:4 teaches, "I sought the Lord, and He answered me, And delivered me from all my fears." Did you notice that before the Lord delivers us from our fears, we must seek Him? In Hebrew, the word *pursue* can be used for *sought*. A synonym for *pursuing* is "running after" or "chasing." This paints a very clear picture of our responsibility.

If we want to be FearLESS, we must run after God and chase Him with all our heart, mind, and soul. In our heart, we must determine, as Daniel did, not to defile ourselves. In our mind, we must meditate on the Word of God day and night, as Psalm 1:2 instructs us. Finally, in our soul, the seat of our emotions, we must daily bring our emotions in line with God's Word. As a result, we will not get tossed to and fro. As Ephesians 4:14 tells us, "We are no longer to be children, tossed here and there by waves, and carried about by every wind of doctrine, by the trickery of men."

Once we become men and women who chase after the Lord, we will be men and women who fear the Lord. When we fear God and not man, we will view the world through a different lens—God's lens. Our perspective will change. We will be more concerned about God's opinion than man's. Our earthly fears will diminish as we turn our trust and reliance to Him.

Marta

Reflection

What manifestation of fear, such as anxiety or insomnia, particularly bothers you?

Have your fears diminished in the past twenty-four days of this study?

In what ways has God been strengthening your faith?

Day Twenty Five

The Same God

So I will choose their punishments,

and I will bring on them what they dread.

Because I called, but no one answered; I spoke, but they did not listen.

And they did evil in My sight, and chose that in which I did not delight.

Isaiah 66:4

Isaiah was a prophet to the nation of Judah...

... the Southern Kingdom, from 739–681 BC. There are sixty-six books in the Bible, and there are a total of sixty-six chapters in the book of Isaiah. The verse listed here is in the final chapter of Isaiah and issues a profound warning to every person ever born.

The previous verse (Isa. 66:3) outlines things people choose to do in their own way that are not at all pleasing to God and says "their soul delights in their abominations." Because they choose their own steps, God promises to choose their punishments and bring on them what they dread.

Here's the deal: God is the same yesterday and today. God's words were true in 730 BC and true today. The same God who warned the Israelites is warning the nations today. He judged the people then for taking things into their own hands, and he will judge us in this century for going against His commandments. God, through Isaiah, is warning the nations to hear His Word, to glorify Him, and to honor Him above all things.

The definition of dread is "great fear." This devotional includes stories of the authors' own encounters with great fear. I believe nothing any of us has gone through in life will be as dreadful as the judgment that will surely come if the world does not change its course and return to God.

The Lord is warning us of the consequences if we do not change our ways. What we fear (dread) the most will happen. He is God, El Shaddai, God Almighty, and He is sovereign. He was distressed by sin in Old Testament times, and I believe He is distressed with the world today.

There is only one way to truly be FearLESS: by looking to and following the one true God and living with His Son, Jesus, as our example.

Reflection

Is there something specific you are dreading today?

What is your plan to find peace and feel safe in the midst of your fear?

How will you pray for our nation today?

SECTION TWO

New Testament

Dēiliaō

δειλι

"John 14:27 is the only time in the New Testament this Greek word is used. It simply means to be timid or fearful."[14]

---

[14] "Deiliao meaning in Bible," accessed April 5, 2021, https://www.biblestudytools.com/lexicons/greek/nas/deiliao.html.

Day Twenty Six

The Gift of Peace

Peace I leave with you;

My peace I give to you; not as the world gives, do I give to you.

Let not your heart be troubled, nor let it be fearful.

John 14:27

Jesus explained to his disciples that He would be leaving (John 14).

We, of course, know that Jesus would suffer unbearably and be crucified for our sins, buried, and—the most amazing miracle of all—resurrected on the third day. After some time passed, He would then ascend into heaven. The disciples did not know the future, nor did they have Scripture to reveal what was going to happen.

What do you believe the disciples were thinking, and how do you think it made them feel when Jesus told them He was leaving but would send a "helper"? I would have been very confused. What is He talking about? Why is He leaving us? Where is He going? Who is coming to be the helper?

Have you ever felt the way the disciples may have been feeling—that something is a little "off"? Are you unsettled? In today's troubling times, it is easy to think *I just need some peace*. Jesus understood the disciples must have been concerned about the same thing.

In John 14:27, Jesus says, "Peace I leave with you; My peace I give you; not as the world gives, do I give to you. Let not your heart be troubled, nor let it be fearful." The words "Peace be with you," or "shalom," was a common phrase people used in greeting or departure. Jesus

was getting His disciples ready for His return to the Father and wanted them to know He was giving them a gift unattainable by the world—His peace. Remember, friends, if we are His disciples, we too have all been bestowed with this gift. Call on Jesus in times of fear, and His peace will descend on you! I pray you have a life of His peace! Shalom.

Reflection

In what ways is your world or the world a little "off" today?

....
....
....
....
....
....

What can you do to get things back in balance?

....
....
....
....
....

In which areas of your life are you asking for God's peace?

....
....
....
....

Mērimnaō

μεριμνάω

"This Greek word is only used 17 times in the New Testament. It simply means to be anxious or troubled with cares."[15]

---

[15] "Merimnao Meaning in Bible," accessed April 5, 2021, www.biblestudytools.com/lexicons/greek/nas/merimnao.html.

The Day the Earth Moved

My Story

I used to live in Southern California, the land of the sudden surprises called earthquakes. One Sunday morning, I was awakened around five o'clock by a 6.9 magnitude earthquake that shook the house and sent me flying out of bed. Fortunately, everything appeared undamaged. I was settling outside on the patio to have a cup of tea when the ground began to shake again. This time, I watched while the brick chimney on my house crumbled to the ground and the sliding glass door popped out of its frame as the house moved. The ground looked like an ocean of waves as it rolled toward the house. This was a 7.3, and it was *scary*! Every item in my house that was not nailed down fell to the ground. The cupboards flew open, and every glass and plate and cup lay shattered on the floor. The refrigerator and freezer doors opened, and a sea of milk and mustard and ketchup mixed with the glass on the floor. Closet shelves emptied, their contents piling onto the floor. We were fortunate that our house was still standing and stable.

Thousands of aftershocks follow a large earthquake. I was very fearful every time the ground moved. Would windows break? Would the roof stay in place? Were my children safe in their bedrooms?

It took a couple of days to get the initial mess all cleaned up, and I was beginning to become comfortable in my home again when a 5.0 magnitude aftershock occurred. Everything we had put away or replaced again tumbled to the floor. We camped outside for a few nights to make sure the house was stable, and it took a few months before I felt secure in my own home again and no longer lived in fearful anticipation of another earthquake.

I saw the hand of God during this season in the people who comforted each other. I saw the hand of God in those who took in strangers who needed a place to sleep. I saw the hand of God in the houses that were not destroyed and the lives that were spared.

The future is uncertain every single day. We do not know what type of "earthquake" will hit us—car accident, illness, death of a loved one, or a pandemic. I learned that we need to let go of the anticipation of that fear so it does not steal the joy that is right in front of us. Believers are not called to walk in fear; they are called to walk in faith and be FearLESS.

Day Twenty Seven

Anxiety

Be anxious for nothing,

but in everything by prayer and supplication

with thanksgiving let your requests be made known to God.

Philippians 4:6

Jesus was well aware that life was not easy.

Every person experiences difficulty of some type and resultant fear. Our Savior understood we may be anxious or fearful in tough times but wants us to be FearLESS in Him. Philippians 4:6–7 tells us to "[b]e anxious for nothing, but in everything by prayer and supplication with thanksgiving let your requests be made known to God. And the peace of God, which surpasses all comprehension, will guard your hearts and minds in Christ Jesus." Jesus did not mean we should rejoice about the tragedies in life, but He was teaching us to keep our eyes focused on the Lord, no matter what.

Anxiety is a form of fear. Do you ever wake up just feeling anxious or fearful? Are you fearful of what the day may bring or fearful of how you will react to something? The enemy will use any number of ways to get to you and steal your peace. I am ever amazed at the unlimited wisdom of a God who knows we can't always "handle the truth"—but He can. We just need to recognize the fear we are feeling, figure out how we can be thankful in the situation, and then give it to God. He's got it!

Is this easy? Absolutely not! Does this mean the tragedy or trial will go away? Probably not. Is it possible to rejoice in every situation? Absolutely. We may not be able to praise Him for allowing something to happen, but we can praise Him for being God and being present with us. We can look to a beautiful sunset and thank Him for that in the midst of a storm. We need to keep our focus on the One who shares His peace with us no matter what life brings. Give all your fears to Him this week!

Reflection

Recall a time when you were able to praise God in the midst of a trial.

....

....

....

....

....

....

How did it help your faith?

....

....

....

....

How did it reveal faith to others?

....

....

....

....

Phŏbĕ

φοβέω

φοβέω **phŏbĕō**, *fob-eh´-o*; from *5401*; to *frighten*, i.e., (pass.) to *be alarmed*; by anal. to *be in awe* of — i.e., *revere*:—be (+ sore) afraid, fear (exceedingly), reverence. This word is used ninety-three times in the New Testament.

> Expressions containing words of the φόβος group always describe a reaction to man's encounter with force. The scale of reactions ranges from spontaneous terror and anxiety to honour and respect, which already presupposes mastery of the experience through reflection. Hence evaluation of the reaction of fear is closely bound up with the understanding of one's own existence. It also offers access to the religious self-understanding of specific individuals and groups.[17]

---

[16] J. Strong, *A Concise Dictionary of the Words in the Greek Testament and The Hebrew Bible*, vol. 1 (Bellingham, WA: Logos Bible Software, 2009), 76.

[17] H. Balz & G. Wanke (1964–), φοβέω, φοβέομαι φόβος, δέος. *Theological Dictionary of the New Testament,* electronic edition., vol. 9, ed. G. Kittel, G. W. Bromiley, & G. Friedrich (Chicago: Moody Press, 1999), 192.

Blessings on the Porch

My Story

As the second of seven children, I enjoyed a childhood full of people, love, and activity. My parents worked hard to supply our needs, but we learned that hard work was necessary if we had any specific wants. When I was twelve years old, my father was chronically ill and unable to work. My mother worried constantly over how she was going to provide enough food to feed her sick husband and seven children. My mom could stretch a half-pound of hamburger meat in many creative ways to fill our bellies.

I still have a clear picture in my mind of waking up one morning to hear my mother crying. I was afraid something had happened to my father, but she was crying tears of joy! She told me, "Look outside!" Our porch, which stretched the length of the house, was completely covered with brown bags filled with groceries. We never knew exactly who had brought over the food, but it turned out that the people who had worked with my father had gotten together, bought groceries, and snuck them over during the night.

This good deed got us through until my father was able to get back to work, and it completely eased my mother's burden of *phobeo* (fear).

Maureen

Day Twenty Eight

No Hostages

Do not be afraid, little flock,

for your Father has chosen gladly to give you the kingdom.

Luke 12:32

We are all a part of the "little flock"...

... Jesus mentions in Luke 12:32 when He tells them, "Do not be afraid." Jesus told his disciples not to be anxious about what they would eat or wear. In Luke 12:24, Jesus compares us to birds, saying we are more valuable than ravens, and look how well they are cared for. We are not to worry or be afraid of what life will bring us.

It is easy to have no fear when life is going smoothly and very difficult when serious problems arise, such as health scares, financial woes, relationship disasters, and the death of loved ones. How do we trust God and learn to live FearLESS during these times?

Do not let fear hold you hostage. Here is a list of things that help me:

1) Put God in your mind and heart by studying His Word and devoting time every day to just Him.

2) Recall the times God has come to your rescue, the times he has proven He was there and answered prayer.

3) Worship God with joy; listen to and sing praise music.

4) Be thankful for what you *do* have, even in times of distress (food, clothing, water, air, etc.)

5) Be aware that things will come against you to try to keep you from trusting God.

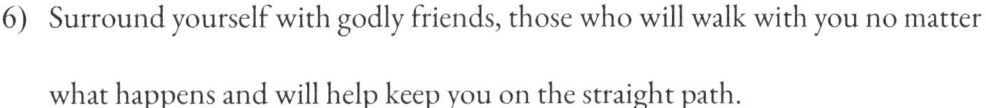

6) Surround yourself with godly friends, those who will walk with you no matter what happens and will help keep you on the straight path.

7) Seek the peace that can come only from God. Find Scriptures that talk of His peace (there are many!).

Those who have trust in the Lord will not live in fear. Be like the ravens and do not be afraid. Trust in God, knowing He will take care of you.

Maureen

Reflection

Can you say, "I am no longer hostage to fear"?

Why or how?

What especially helps you when fear comes?

Day Twenty Nine

Jesus Holds the Keys

*When I saw Him, I fell at His feet as a dead man.
And He laid His right hand upon me,
saying, "Do not be afraid; I am the first and the last,
and the living One; and I was dead,
and behold, I am alive forevermore,
and I have the keys of death and of Hades."*
Revelation 1:17–18

*W*e see the power of God and His Son revealed in Revelation 1.

John describes Jesus as the firstborn of the dead, the ruler of the kings of the earth, and the One who is alive forevermore. His voice is like the sound of a trumpet, booming and powerful. Jesus's eyes are flames of fire and His feet burnished bronze. Out of His mouth comes a two-edged sword.

When John sees Jesus, he immediately falls at His feet. How does Jesus respond? He says, "Do not be afraid," and explains why he is not to be afraid.

Jesus tells John He holds the keys of death and Hades. What did that mean to John, and ultimately, what does it mean to you and me? Satan's goal is to steal, kill, and destroy our lives (John 10:10). But if we are children of the living King, we don't fear the schemes and destruction of the enemy, because Jesus bought and paid for us. He holds the keys of death and Hades. We are secure in our Lord's

grip. Jesus says, "My sheep hear My voice, and I know them, and they follow Me; and I give eternal life to them, and they shall never perish; and no one will snatch them out of My hand" (John 10:27–28). Jesus's grip is  strong and secure. We don't need to trust in ourselves to hold on to Jesus because He is holding on to us.

Satan can do nothing to change our eternal destiny. It is sealed when we place our trust in the One who released us from our sins by His own blood. We do not fear death, because Jesus holds the keys.

Marta

Reflection

Do you fear death? What needs to change?

....
....
....
....
....

In what ways are you intently listening to the shepherd's voice?

....
....
....
....
....
....

Does the description of Jesus in Revelation surprise you? How would you describe Him?

....
....
....
....
....

Day Thirty

Be Ready

And the angel said to them, "Do not be afraid."

Luke 2:10

I magine a dark night in a small town called Bethlehem ...

... where outside in the fields, the shepherds were watching their sheep, probably sleeping in shifts. They were just doing their jobs, living ordinary lives. Then out of nowhere, an angel appeared with a "great host" of angelic figures! My hope is that the words "Do not be afraid" really did the trick and the shepherds were able to quiet their instant fear and listen to the angel's message

The first words the angel spoke to the shepherds were "Do not be afraid." Then the exciting news followed: "For behold, I bring you good news of a great joy which shall be for all the people; for today in the city of David there has been born for you a Savior; who is Christ the Lord" (Luke 2:10–11).

The Jewish people had been waiting for the coming of a Savior. God

chose to reveal the message of His arrival to a small group of simple shepherds who knew the prophecies and were faithful in doing their jobs. They were the first ones to hear the wonderful news. A Savior was born for *all* people. He was  here for the humble, the rich, and the poor. He was here for the Jew and the gentile. Those humble shepherds had the honor of hearing the news first, straight from heaven!

God chose to break His good news first to humble shepherds. We need to become more like the shepherds—do our jobs, live our lives, be content, and always be ready to welcome the return of our Savior! *Maureen*

Reflection

Are you in position and ready for the return of Christ?

Do you fear His coming or look forward in faith with FearLESS hope?

How do you imagine you will react when you meet Jesus?

Your Story

We want to know what God has done in your life! Write your testimony here, or send an email to info@wogt.org.

Become a Words of Grace & Truth Supporter

_____ Yes, I want to become a member of the prayer warrior team!

_____ Yes, I would like to become a faithful friend of Words of Grace & Truth and support the ministry financially. I want to help spread His truth to the nations.

_____ Expect a monthly check for $ (e.g., $25, $50, $100, or more). Please make all checks payable to Words of Grace & Truth. You may also make a one-time or recurring donation online at http://www.wogt.org.

_____ Please charge my credit/debit card on the first or fifteenth of each month in the amount of $ (e.g., $25, $50, $100, or more).

_____ Enclosed is my one-time gift to help spread His truth through Words of Grace & Truth.

You can also make a secure online donation at http://www.wogt.org.

We also have a text-to-give number: 75228. Type "GTRW 15" in the comments.

Visa/MasterCard/AMEX/Discover Card #_____

Name: _____

Address: _____

Email Address: _____

Phone Number: (_____) _____-_____

Words of Grace & Truth
PO Box 860223
Plano, TX 75086-0223
Phone: 469-854-3574

"And blessed be His glorious name forever; and may the whole earth be filled with His glory. Amen, and Amen" (Psalm 72:19).

Follow Marta and Maureen on:
Facebook: Words of Grace & Truth
https://www.facebook.com/profile.php?id=100064809695832
Instagram: WordsofGraceAndTruth
Maureen Herman Maldonado
Twitter: Marta E Greenman @WordsofGraceTruth
Linkedin: Marta Greenman
Maureen Maldonado

Please direct request for all additional copies to
Words of Grace & Truth, PO Box 860223, Plano, TX 75086
www.wogt.org | 1-800-257-1626 or 469-854-3574

If you enjoyed this devotional and found it to be helpful to your spiritual life please go to Amazon and leave a review.

Made in the USA
Monee, IL
18 October 2023

44766764R00096